Women Are Our Only Hope

(Because Men Have Proven To Be Unfit To Lead Us.)

Anthony DiGiorgio

authorHOUSE™

1663 LIBERTY DRIVE, SUITE 200
BLOOMINGTON, INDIANA 47403
(800) 839-8640
WWW.AUTHORHOUSE.COM

First published by AuthorHouse 2/8/2006

ISBN: 1-4208-8468-9 (sc)

Printed in the United States of America
Bloomington, Indiana

This book is printed on acid-free paper.

Cover design and illustration by Andrew Holahan, amhdesign.com

This book was edited by Christine Holahan, who says she may not agree with what I say but will make certain I say it correctly.

Other works by author
A letter to god
The naked cynic
Oh my Papa
A Mothers choice
Smart ships are not the answer

Author website:
Writerofwrongs.com

This book is dedicated to the mothers of those killed or scarred for life in body or soul, by war, poverty, caste, crime, and disease.

Knowledge breeds freedom.
Religion breeds contempt, ignorance, and hate.

Sadly most humans feel religious.

Prologue

Here is how men treat women:

Women are not allowed to publicly expose any part of their
    bodies in some countries.
Women are stoned to death for adultery in some countries,
    while men are allowed to have multiple wives.
Wives are burned alive in some countries, so that the hus-
    bands can marry again for better dowries.
Women cannot have an abortion unless men legislate it.
Women cannot preach in most religions throughout the
    world.
Women cannot legislate war, yet must provide sons and
    daughters to fight and die in these wars.
Women rarely become leaders of countries.
Women do not make the same money as men even when
    doing the same work.
Women do more work than men in most countries of the
    world.
Women's genitals are mutilated in some countries to prevent
    their enjoying sexual intercourse due to tradition.

And this is the way it is with the most sophisticated mammal
on earth.

To think that we, the men, think of ourselves as the fair and
just providers and defenders of the race.

On the other end, what if women took half of the time they
spend in adorning themselves and invested it in achieving equality?

Hitler is quoted: *What luck for rulers that men do not think.*
One could say: *What luck for men that most women do not complain.*

Women are our only hope to make this earth a better place for all species because we, the men, are not fit to lead humanity.

During the last 50 centuries of recorded civilization we, the men, have suppressed women, raped the environment, killed each other, created temporary true gods and rationalized all we did not want or could not understand as the will of these gods.

Women, during the same time period, have obeyed not only the commands of men, but have even gone along with the thousands of religions which men found necessary to create. While being in the background of mankind, women did all of the work that men found demeaning and more importantly provided raw meat for the wars that old men start but which require youngsters to fight and suffer horrible deaths.

A contemporary example of the submissiveness of women can be found in America:

America, a democracy on paper, has during the last 230 years of existence suffered at least one million battlefield deaths. Whereas women literally bred each of those dead soldiers, they had no legal say-so on sending them to die. This is due to the fact that somehow American women are prevented from full participation in the American Government. This is true, because during the entire existence of America there have been over 11,000 elected Congressmen, 216 of which were/are women. Yet only women provided the soldiers. Think about what happens in other governments where women have even less rights.

The issue is simple: Men advance civilization with the agility of sloths and destroy it with the power and grace of stampeding elephants. Women, on the other hand, are not allowed to participate in the leadership of humanity, but they must provide the men to do such things.

Women are kept away from participating in the decision making processes of civilizations by many tacitly accepted traditional norms. One needs only look at our manly ignorance to begin to understand the stupidity of our traditions. In the world of mammals breast feeding is a natural part of feeding the young. Yet, in America, the country that can send people to the moon and bring them back alive, a lactating woman cannot breast feed her young in a public place. American men make it their responsibility to enact laws to allow/prohibit such a simple and natural event. Of course there are masculine reasons for this, stupidity being at the forefront.

Women, most anyway, have embraced such servitude as a norm. How else can one explain women obediently providing sons and daughters to die in wars, wars started by men, and accepting ceremonial flags as replacements for their losses? Is there a truer testament of women's enslavement to men?

Whereas it is a norm for us men to be as we are, why do women go along with it? We, the men, think it vulgar to show humans having sex in the art world. Remember that recent defender of the law who put a drape on the breasts of a statue? But it is okay, and believed to be patriotic, to train a young man or woman to kill and at times actually see them being killed in combat.

How unnatural can we be?

Whereas the majority of men and women go along with any local tradition and complain only when they do not have freedom from fear or a warm place to eat and defecate, within each of us there is always hope of a better world for our children.

This is why we send our kids to school.

The majority of the time we encourage our children to higher education than we achieved, because our heartfelt belief is that there is a better life or a better way. The only exception is for the children of politicians.

Through the years a handful of women have stepped out of the male imposed bondages and fought for equality. The freedoms that women enjoy today were achieved by those few women who questioned the norms and changed them whenever they could. Those few equalities enjoyed by women were never given to them by men out of a pure sense of equality.

Any future freedom or equality sought by women will be achieved only by women who will struggle for it. Man, God, Nature have not and will not give you equality.

If women were to achieve equality, the world would be a better place. It is a fact that women give birth to mankind and do not go around killing the children of other mothers.

You, the women, are our only hope to get us men off of this vehicle of war and hate. You have the option to continue as if you were dogs under the tables waiting for scraps. Then rationalize it as a great achievement when we men throw you a bone with some meat on it. Alternatively, you can stop us traditional men by beginning to make us change our ways, admit our faults and share the leadership with women as equal partners.

You are not equal to men. You are better, but yet your sensitivity and femininity has kept you a slave to the brute force masculine mentality that rules the world. In time it will be shown that you are more peaceful than men and a better civilizer than men.

The following ideas, which are offered as kindling to those of you who want to improve the wellbeing of all could be the beginning of discourses for equality in humanity.

You can achieve equality, only when you realize that you are not being treated as an equal, and that you are the only one who is going to make changes.

Criticism is the mother of progress. Therefore look at your social standing and criticize it, and from that criticism equality will be born.

Start by getting together with other women and admit that you have had enough. Unite with other women of the world and use whatever legal, physical, financial, and even emotional means that are necessary to achieve equal rights.

You need to decide whether your sons and daughters suffer or die in a ghetto, barrio, battlefield, or perhaps live a hopeful life, regardless of social standing.

If you, women, do not start to change the world, your daughters will live as you have. Your traditional submissiveness is the cause of your lower status in this manly world.

Accept no substitute for equality.

Here is some kindling. You get some wood and matches. Then light the fires which can liberate you from your present status.

THE MIND IS THE ANSWER

Convince the leaders of the world to invest money and time in researching how human minds work. Make this the highest human goal. This will take a few generations, but once begun it will start to provide results as it progresses and will lessen the need of wars, killing, and seemingly natural occurring diseases. To achieve this, convince the leaders to take half of the defense budget to fund the program. This will be the best defense for America and the world

TEACH THEM POOR KIDS
WITH THE BEST YOU GOT

Turn the Naval Academy into a training school for teachers. Train these teachers to be superior to any of the present teachers who enter that profession. The student teachers would be selected on a random basis, based on grades and then fed, housed, and treated as the present naval cadets are treated. The candidates must be selected from students who have at least a B average in classes that include math, physics, literature, liberal arts, but no sports or other physical activities. Once out of the teachers academy they would be offered jobs teaching in the poorest school districts and paid twice the national average pay for teachers. As long as they remain active teachers in poor school districts they would always receive twice as much as other school teachers.

PAY THE TEACHERS NOT THE PRINCIPALS

Reverse the present process where school administrators make more money than school teachers do. A school principal should make less than a school teacher, on an average basis. Achieve this by first having a national study of the present school administration processes and then modifying the present system.

GROWING LEADERS INSTEAD OF GETTING MORONS FROM TEXAS AND CALIFORNIA

Turn the Air Force Academy into a school that trains leaders. Similar to the teachers academy, pay the students, and teach them about managing people, cities, counties, states, and countries. Our present selection of leaders is archaic and illogical. You would never go to a doctor who has learned medicine by dabbling in it, so why have idiots lead you? The future leaders need to be educated in matters that affect civilizations, such as, leadership, sociology, and economy. The student leaders must live overseas with local families and work for local governments for an entire year, preferably in underdeveloped countries. The graduates of these schools would become city managers, mayors, state and federal representatives, and of course president. This should prevent the installing of another idiot in the White House. Accept foreign students from third world countries into this leadership school, so that they can seed the new governments in their nations.

ELECTIONS OF PRESIDENTS AND OTHER HIGH OFFICIALS

Presently the process of electing leaders is either a beauty contest or a forced feeding of propaganda to the masses. The American expenditures for the election of 2004 were 50 times more than the job would pay for its duration. Do you know of any American so dumb as to pay such a high price for a job and get 1 penny back on every 50 cents? The election should be modified to a secret questioning of all candidates by 100 members of the intelligentsia and 50 members from business and 50 members from the working stiffs. After the questioning, the entire recorded event would be played on public television around the clock, for one month prior to the election. Let the people make up their minds based on unassisted, off the cuff answers to 200 unique questions asked by randomly picked Americans.

WHERE DID THAT HAMBURGER COME FROM

Have all food processing industries install live cameras at their farms, factories and dispensing places, so that anyone can see how a cow is fed, butchered, and cooked. Of course tell everyone, pictorially, what is inside a hot dog . Imagine seeing the process which turns some animal parts into ham, or so called turkey breast, and trying to figure out if there really is any namesake meat in the final product.

MINIMIZE THEM LAWS

Establish federal and state commissions to evaluate our legal systems, and begin to streamline them.

TO KILL THE KILLERS IS DUMB

Abolish the death penalty. Someday the conservatives will understand that an eye for an eye begets you partial or full blindness, not justice, and that their Christ was the first Bleeding Heart Liberal.

RICH BOYS LIVE IN THE BARRIOS/GHETTOS FOR A WHILE

Establish a national student exchange program for 17 year olds. For one year the rich kids will live with the family of poor kids and vice versa. A simple way is to establish a mandatory exchange of students on the basis of widest income disparity. Once you get to the middle class, where the money is equal, then go on the basis of races and ethnicity.

NESTING PERIODS

Too many children are raised in dysfunctional families and suffer adulthood problems because of it. The idea of marriage as it has existed throughout the world does not work. It is time to consider changing it. One way would be to establish a nesting period, a contract between heterosexual or homosexual couples and the state. It would allow the making of only one child but adoption of as many as desired. The nesting contract will describe home discipline, schooling on any voluntary aspect of raising children who can sustain themselves during their adulthood. The qualifications to enter a nesting period will require schooling on how to raise children, and a deposit of earnest money, equal to one month's salary into a national insurance fund. The insurance fund is to be used for cases where one parent dies or deserts the agreement. Upon rearing a child to 18 years of age, if the nesting couple did not take any assistance from the insurance fund then the money plus any earnings are returned to the couple, or used for educating the child past basic schooling.

YOU CAN PLAY BUT YOU WON'T MAKE A BABY

Insert birth control capsules in the bodies of post-pubescent boys and girls, and remove them only when they accept the responsibilities of having children. These birth control devices cannot be removed until they decide to enter the nesting period.

ONE COUPLE, ONE CHILD

Enact international laws where any nesting couple can have only one live birth. Do this until the world population reaches 2 billion people. After that go back to 2 children, but never above it. There is no need to have 7 billion starving, killing, and polluting humans roam the earth and make life miserable for all the other earthlings.

HEY JUDGE

Stop the American tradition of calling a sitting judge, "your honor." There really is no need for that assignment of respect to a human.

YOUR CHILD WILL SURVIVE

In the underdeveloped countries entice nesting couples to have only one child by providing medical and nutritional assistance to insure that the child would survive to adulthood. Another possibility is to offer physical methods of birth prevention, in exchange for housing or long term medical, educational and nutritional assistances to nesting couples who have opted to have only one child.

TELL THE CHILDREN ABOUT THE LAWS

Children are not citizens of a country until they reach the age of 18, and show comprehension of the social issues. The schooling of children should involve a minimum of one hour per school day of civil obedience. This course will progress as the student ages and will include ethical and legal training. When the child reaches the age of 18 he/she should be fully aware of the consequences of disobeying the laws of the lands where he/she lives.

HELP THEM RAISE THEIR KID

Develop videos, online instant assistance agencies, discussion panels of nesting parents, and whatever else is necessary to train nesting parents on how to raise children. Establish a social guide on how parents are to be punished when they let their little bundles run wild, especially in places where others do not find it joyous to see these two legged generators of noise and feces make fair minded adults wonder where the disconnect between courtesy and freedom lies. Also have the videos explain the different phases that children go through, and thus hope that instead of a parent shaking a child to death, or leaving it with older siblings to burn to death in a house, or to be stifled to death in a hot auto, she/he may be better educated to care for the child.

IT'S TIME TO DIE

Develop a voluntary rating system which older people can use to make decisions on when they want to die. Individuals, between the ages of 50-60 years, should be encouraged and assisted in scoping out ways on how they want to end their lives. The present hanging on as guinea pigs for the medical profession is truly a most inhumane way of living. One possibility is to develop a system of assigning personally chosen values for the type of old age that each individual wants to live. Establish a LIFE VALUE INDEX, where people can assign their own cutoff value. Here are some present thoughts on the importance of certain human faculties that I value:

Disease - Disability	Value
Unable to walk	10
Unable to care for self	50
Loss of mind	100
Incontinence	60
Unable to feed self	20
Blindness/deafness	10
Terminal diseases	100

The elder individual would assign a value to diseases or physical disabilities that he/she feels not worth experiencing and then set a cutoff point. For me the moment I get to a value of 60 or more, it would be time to go. Develop a legal process where a legal executor of the will has the power to go on with the process in case of comatose or other mentally disabling diseases. Once the value is achieved, the individual will opt for death. The individual will celebrate the last day in whatever mode was chosen. Then he/she is administered a sleeping pill which kills.

OLD MEN DECLARE WAR AND GO TO WAR

Have another Geneva Convention on war and change the global rules about war, including the constitution of the armies. Make it so that a country can raise an army consisting only of people age 60 or older. Since the older people have already enjoyed the benefits of a country and they owe the country, they are obligated to pay for it. The present use of youths to defend the old is a barbaric process. A youth has not enjoyed the fruits of his/her country and should not be allowed to go die so that the old farts, the ones who started the wars, can sit at home and justify their ineptitude at getting along with all. If the old people want war, let them go fight it. This may sound ridiculous, but if we, the older men who wave the flag while youths slaughter each other, had any self respect and sense of common good, we would change the process and go pay for what we believe in, versus having kids die for it.

PROPAGANDA IN AMERICA

In a democracy propaganda is to freedom what pneumonia is to a very old person. To call terrorists cowards and praise some of our fighters who kill from 500 miles away is simply propaganda. Stop these abuses.

NO HEROES HERE

To have a government make heroes out of people who die while doing their jobs is propaganda. Police, firemen, school crossing guards, and so on may die on their jobs. It is part of it. Again, rebel against this, since it is an insult to your intelligence.

THE BELIEVERS ARE THE PROBLEM

One thousand years ago the Christians slaughtered the Muslims and called it the Crusades. Actually the crusaders slaughtered anyone thought to be Muslim, like we killed anyone who looked like a Vietcong, or presently a terrorist ...., Now the Muslims are slaughtering the non-believers, and calling it Jihad. It is up to you to teach your children the stupidity of religion, and hopefully prevent repeats of our killing phases. Peaceful people change the world. Generals kill. Vemon spouting religious leaders instill hate in the hearts of simple men. Therefore, Mothers of the world, the makers of future leaders, you need to instill in your young that war is vulgar, and religious wars happen only for those who are gullible to believe that their god or religion is worth preserving.

FOR THE COMMON FOLK

Create a monument with the names of simple citizens who obeyed the laws and tried in whichever way they could to better the well-being of all species. Exclude all politicians and government workers from such a monument.

YOU SIN, YOU PAY

Rethink the present imprisonment of convicts. One option is to not differentiate between the type of crimes committed by first offenders. First offenders should be forced into a period of psychological conditioning. If the individual becomes a second time offender, then consider lobotomy.

WHEN NO MEANS NEVER AGAIN

Rapists, once proven to be so without any doubt, should be sexually neutered, either physically or chemically.

YOU ARE DEAD, YOU ARE GONE

Convince people to have their remains incinerated, or whichever means of disposal is least polluting. There is no greater act of disrespect of nature than having one's remains become a testament to nothing. One way to achieve this would be to create a monument for non-polluters, and add the names of people who opted for the least polluting way of disposing of their remains.

NO DRAFT NO SERVICEMEN

Do not refer to present day US military personnel as servicemen. The people in the military today are there because they chose it and are paid rather well. They are employees, just like anyone else. The WWII and all of the other draftees were servicemen.

PAYING THEIR WORTH

Make it so that the president of the United States and the governors and mayors of states and cities are paid salaries much higher than they are presently paid. However, at the beginning of each year, each citizen is made to vote a pass/fail ballot on the job performance of the official. Pay the official the same percentages of the high salary as that decided by the populaces.

FAT CATS AT CIVIL SERVICE

Abolish all the exorbitant benefits that government workers, including presidents, congressmen, and judges receive, except for those given to school teachers, firemen and policemen. Of course you can always legislate benefits similar to government workers for the working stiffs who work outside the castles of governments and cannot afford medical/retirement benefits as the inside the castle people.

THE FATTER YOU ARE THE MORE YOU POLLUTE

Advertise how much energy/pollution a human converts each day and based on that make people eat less and pollute less.

WHAT'S ON THAT PLATE

Make restaurants list the chemical and caloric contents of prepared meals on the menu, so that a patron knows what is being eaten.

SPEAK THE LINGO

Establish an international language, which uses words that are logical and extracted from each present language. Teach this international language on the same basis as the local language to each new human. This should stop the present confusion of translating some city names, or not knowing that the plural of concerto is concerti, not concertos.

KIDS ARE NOT BORN EVIL

In all of the schools teach children the necessity to get along and not discriminate against anyone because of physical makeup, nationality, or religious beliefs.

PAY THE FULL BUCK

Stop the American idiotic way of selling any item for values which are short of the whole number; e.g., instead of selling something for $4.95, it must be sold for $5. This will show respect for human intelligence and will also be easier to enter into the accounting systems.

IT'S USED

Abolish the traditional and accepted lies that exist in American businesses. There should never be any words like, "previously owned cars", a house that is a "fixer-up", or any small writing at the end of the contract.

METERS LITERS KILOS

Change the American measurements system to the metric system. I do not know why businessmen have not discovered the simple fact that if we want to sell to the rest of the world, the least we can do is give them products, tools, and machines that conform to their measuring system. Likewise, if we want the foreigners to spend money in our country, we might as well tell them the distance between two cities in kilometers.

LET'S DRIVE TO PERU

Build a highway system between North and South America so that someone from eastern or western Canada can go all the way down to southern Argentina and southern Peru.

NO UNEMPLOYED

All nations must have full employment for their citizens. Migration can be allowed only on a reciprocal basis. When a government cannot feed and educate its citizens, then the names of the leaders of that country should be entered on the Wall of Shame Monument.

EQUAL PAY

Women must be paid the same as men for any similar work. No exceptions.

EQUIVALENT BODY EXPOSURE

Women should educate themselves to dress similarly to men. If men go without clothing on some parts of their bodies, so will women. Inversely, in an office a man shows only his neck and hands, whereas a woman shows her breasts, legs, arms, and whatever other parts "fashion" dictates. WHY?

MUTILATION OF WOMEN

Women cannot be genitally MUTILATED because of religion or tradition. If they are, then the leaders of that government must also be similarly mutilated.

KILLING/ABORTING BABIES
ON A GENDER BASIS

Countries which prize babies of one sex above the other need to be exposed and financially boycotted until the tradition is stopped.

ABORTION

should be made available to any woman who wants it.

WAR BAD, HOMESEXUALITY OKAY

Teach all earthlings that war is vulgar, and sexual deeds between consenting adults are acceptable.

HAVING THE RICH LIVE AS PAUPERS

The rich people of any country must be made to spend one month per year with the poorest people of that country. Similar to exchange students, the rich people need to live and eat with a poor family to better understand the results of simple ideas like minimum wages, poverty levels, and all of those neat expressions that somehow hide the reality of poverty. During that month period, the rich fellow cannot contact anyone from their normal rich life, and if violated, then the time doubles.

CLEAN SHOPPING CARTS

American business places which offer shopping carts must teach their pimple faced cart gatherers to clean the carts of refuse before making them available to new shoppers.

LEGALIZE DRUGS

Legalize all forms of entertainment drugs and sell them in pharmacies. However, take children to hospitals and drug treatment centers and let them see the suffering addicts. Use all net proceeds from selling these drugs to educate all on the problems of drug use and abuse.

GET RID OF THE NUCLEAR STUFF

Dismantle all nuclear weapons and power plants. Do this as an act of love for your descendants.

STOP THE LEGAL DRUGGING OF AMERICANS.

Stop overmedicating Americans.

ABANDONED CHILDREN

Publish data on abandoned children throughout the world. Make this data available to all in hope that others can help.

CURBING THE ABUSES OF SAVED ONES

Establish the sentiment that religion is a belief and that anyone who practices religion has a right to do so, but has no right to approach any other human on the merits of that religion.

GOVERNMENT AND GOD HAVE SEPARATE AGENDA

Separate the government from any religious institution. First, remove all references to God from everyday business, and later, teach children in schools about the various religions and how they have existed throughout time.

DEMISTIFYING THE UNKNOWN

Make every 18 year old human write down at least 100 questions that he/she has about anything. One or two of those questions will be about God and our purpose here. Point out that the questions about God and the reason for our being here are only two of the 100 questions, and the other 98 questions will probably have more important effects on their lives than will the two eternally asked questions..

STOP THE RACE/GENDER HATE

Teach the people of each country the worthiness of each human and in so doing stop the discrimination against race and gender. There have been many non-WASP women who have lived and died who would have been better presidents than most male WASP presidents.

SEX IS GREAT

Educate people that sex is a pleasure, and whereas no one has the right to tell any adult how to drink a beer, neither has anyone the right to tell any adult how to have sex behind closed doors.

THE RETIRED MILITARY

No retired US military person can work for any organization that is involved with the defense or administration of the country.

REARING YOUR OWN CHILD

Once a nesting couple has a child, one parent must stay home with the child until that child reaches an age of maturity, which is to be determined by those who deal with human behavior.

VALUE ADDED TAX

Replace the presently unfair to the rich taxing system with a Value Added Tax, with no exemptions.

MAKING KIDS GROW UP

All children prior to achieving citizenship of their country must witness the places where their governments keep prisoners, treat drug dependant people, and where poor people live in squalor.

JOHNNY GOT HIS GUN

Until the age of the military is changed, all youths that are made to go to war must read books such as: *Johnny Got His Gun, All Quite on The Western Front*, or similar books that their culture has produced.

UNIVERSAL WALL OF SHAME

Establish a Wall of Shame Monument, first on the internet and then in granite. Do this for each country of the world whose citizens elect to do so. For the USA put the names of every US Congressmen, presidents, ambassadors, admirals and generals in office from Sept 11, 1991 to Sept 11, 2001. Add to that list the name of Bin Laden, Sharon, Arafat, and all other people who have allowed the killing of others for the sake of their goals. Each year add the names of leaders who have opted for world violence versus peace and diplomacy.

MOTHERS OF DEAD CHILDREN CONFERENCE

Establish a global Mothers of Dead Children organization. The purpose of this organization is to unite the mothers of the world whose offspring were sent to war or were killed by war, insurrections, revolutions, civil disobedience, gangs, diseases, acts of violence, crime, or poverty. The organization would set rules as to which mothers qualify and enshrine these mothers each year. Each year these women would meet to discuss how to change the world so that the deaths of future children would diminish. The meeting must be held in countries which have achieved the highest survival rates of their children.

THEM KILLING SPORTS

Stop bull fighting, pugilism, hunting, sports fishing, and any other sport where living creatures are killed for the tradition or for the glory of some demented individuals.

POLLUTING LESS

Start awareness campaigns to educate people on how to pollute less. Do we all need a four wheel drive vehicle, in a nation that has 52,000,000 miles of paved roads?

THINK

Teach children to reason and think. Presently there is no such schooling. How else would we have wound up with morons like Reagan, Bush the 1ˢᵗ and 2ⁿᵈ to lead us astray from the basic American concepts?

BABYSITTING GOVERNMENTS

Establish a branch of the UN which will assist people in less developed countries to: establish governments, educate their children on how to survive in the present world, and replace traditional forms of governments which are deemed unfair. It could also take responsibility for the roles where the present tribal governing systems are able to survive the interferences caused by missionaries of our ways.

MORAL CODE

Establish a universal code of morals based on humanity, not religion.

NO LAND MINES

Abolish the use of mines during wars.

WAR IS VULGAR, ONE MORE TIME

Teach children that war is vulgar and that there is no glory in killing or subduing others for reasons created by leaders and soon forgotten.

NO LOBBYING

Stop all lobbying by any organization.

NO COWBOY PRESIDENTS

Teach American leaders that other countries are sovereign regardless of our ability to bomb them.

STAY HOME AND SEE IT ON TV

Install cameras with sound in the wild and other places of interests and provide worldwide broadcasting of it. This will lessen the need of people to go there on tours or "safari", thus keeping the wild, wild.

GOING BACK TO WILDERNESS

Establish procedures to return lands to their natural state, after the human population begins to decrease.

NO, YOU DO NOT HAVE THE RIGHT TO BEAR ARMS

Disarm the citizens to the point where Americans have access to weapons for non-fatal Sporting events but do not have access to them to kill each other or animals.

GUNS DO NOT BUY PROTECTION

The rape of America on 9-11 was not prevented by the most bloated Military Industrial Complex in the world. Neither was it prevented by a citizenry toting over 100,000,000 personal firearms, as directed by the National Rifle Association. But it could have been prevented if we, as Americans, had a soul and treated other nations as such, versus targets of our bombs? Teach your children that killing others is wrong, and killing others with guns or missiles fired from far away is simply cowardice.

CRYSTAL BALLS AND ECONOMISTS

Develop the present art of economics into a science, if possible.

NO SWAT UNITS

Remove SWAT units from American police forces, after you have figured out how the human mind works.

DAILY MEDITATION-EXERCISE

Teach people to spend one hour per day meditating or exercising.

HIGH SCHOOL TO WORK OR COLLEGE

Graduate students from basic schooling with training that either gets them into college or makes them useful employees.

NO MAKEUP FOR WOMEN OR MEN

Teach women to stop prostituting themselves with makeup and revealing clothing. Society is very abusive and mentally deficient on this. You need only observe the way the classic American comic heroes/villains are clothed to see the sexism.

EQUALITY FOR MEN

Make women aware of the simple fact that as long as they keep on marrying men who are taller than they are, they are publicly admitting inferiority.

STREAMLINE THE MILITARY

Change the military from the present multiple commands that do the same thing to one infantry, one air force, one navy, and one uniform.

JURY TRIALS

Get rid of the jury by your peers concept. Replace it with a trial by three judges, or develop a cadre of jurists. The jurists would be graduates with training in law, and their duty would be to see whether the laws were violated, versus being sensitive to how the accused looked/acted. Randomly move the jurors around the country to prevent any human frailty type problems.

NO HIGH SCHOOL SPORTS

Stop the maiming and injuring of young people with competitive sports in schools. Make them compete for the knowledge that will help them, versus for the glamour of victory which vanishes in the minds of fair minded men by the time they reach middle age.

SEX AND CHEERLEADING

Stop having girls show their bodies at cheerleading events. Either dress them as you do boys, or just stop the entire thing. It is sexist.

ALL MEN COULD BE RAPISTS OR MOLESTERS

To believe that only evil or mentally deficient men think of raping or molesting women or young girls is similar to believing that all politicians really care about the welfare of the populace.

Prevent some of the sexual misbehavior problems by repeatedly educating all males on the depravity of sexual abuses.

SPREAD THE MONEY EVENLY

Consider establishing a national failure standard. The aviation industry has a higher safety record than the automobile industry. Whereas we spend billions so that we have only a few hundred Americans killed in airplane accidents per year, we accept the deaths of 30-40,000 Americans who die by auto accident each year. There are thousands of accidents and some which are fatal that occur in the agricultural areas. This does not seem to raise much concern. Why? An accident that kills is an accident that kills, regardless of being in the aviation, construction, agriculture, or automobile industry. Prevent them all, or assign an acceptable tolerance to the processes.

NO COOKIES

Abolish the sale of cookies by girl scouts. Fund such great programs as the Girls and Boys Scout with taxation. It is easier to arm a youth with ideals than to try to reform him as a young adult law breaker.

TEN PERCENT MUST BE SAVED

Teach children to save a minimum of ten percent of their earnings, and 100 percent of fauna and nature.

CROOKED BUSINESSMEN NEED BE PUNISHED

Just as much pain is being inflicted on humans by economics as it is by war. Come up with a universal way of keeping track of crooked businessmen, be they the local official who needs to be bribed, or the CEO of a company who violates laws but is immune to punishment because of political ties.

DEATH IS OKAY

Teach people that dying is part of living. Do this early in the life of all citizens. The idea that we can be saved by drugs is truly a lurid business in its most avaricious form.

THEM FUNERAL DIRECTORS

Regulate the funeral industry. You get less of a raping dealing with a used car salesmen than you do when you deal with those truly inhuman bastards who steal you blindly because you are in an emotional state.

REGULATE THE DRUG BARONS

Regulate the drug industry. They, the drug manufacturers, are the new highway brigands and need to be regulated.

OLD AGE AND WISDOM-DREAM ON

There is no special knowledge acquired by age. Old men can be as stupid as young men, hence teach the younger that assuming that the aged are wise, or need to be respected and obeyed should be based only upon concluding that it is deserved.

RAPE IS A CRIME NOT A SHAME

The hiding of rape victims' names is an insidious process. Rape is not as fatal as murder, but if people keep on treating it as a shameful crime, versus as a crime, it will continue to hold women as the weaker humans. Rape should be treated as a crime and proper punishment dealt to the perpetrators, nothing more or less.

TRADITION KILLS

There are many long term warring disputes which occur on the seams of different religious cults. These disputes can be stopped by forcing the children of the warring parties to attend the same schools where third party teaching staffs try to explain the stupidity of it all.

IGNORANCE IS STILL THE BEST KILLER

Instill in all humans that ignorance is their worst enemy. Religion, racism, ethnicism are accepted forms of ignorance which form the basis of our being the most horrible species on earth. Can you imagine one zebra killing another zebra because it had one too many black stripes?

A MORONIC AMERICA

American democracy could be the greatest achievement of mankind to date if Americans stood up for their rights. Establish a national organization which educates people on their rights and makes the politicians begin to treat Americans as thinkers.

NO PET UNTIL

No family can have a pet until they get training in caring for such a pet. Decrease the population of pets by having people apply for licenses to own a pet.

NEWS WITHOUT BIAS

Our news reporting is a business from which we get controlled news. Establish a public funded news reporting agency and staff it with newly graduated reporters for a maximum of 2 years. Select the editors on a random basis and for temporary periods. Do very little editing and let the neophyte journalists report news that they want to report. This could provide more revealing first person accounts, versus the present "spam and eggs every night."

TOO MANY GENERALS AND ADMIRALS

There are close to 2000 admirals and generals in the US military who receive exorbitant pay/benefit packages. The US Military has won only one real war from 1905 to 2005. Each of these highly paid officers who were on duty during the Rape of America, failed us and should have been sent to a gulag. It is time to streamline the management of the military. Presently each branch of the US military has 9 layers of enlisted and 10 layers of officers. Since three layers of enlisted are also managers, then we have a military that has 6 layers of fodder and 13 layers of leadership. Decrease the number of ranks and the so called "benefits" and increase the pay that each military person receives. Structure the military so that money is paid for knowledge/ability versus the present system of getting more money only by advancing. It's even worse, getting more money while doing the same job, because one is married and has dependents.

THE DOGGIE KEEPS HIS GLANS

Stop the castration and deformation of pets and domesticated animals until we are able to discern how the animals feel about it. We were smart enough to stop castrating humans. Now why not step out of our cocoons of ignorance and dominance and show some feelings for the other species?

HOMOSEXUAL ARE NO DIFFERENT

Stop the hate of homosexuality by explaining to the ignorant masses that no one knows why some people are heterosexual and some are not. Since we do not know how and why we develop sexual tendencies, there is no logic in discriminating against one or the other.

OVERCOMPENSATED CIVIL SERVANT

Again, it is unfair to pay workers differently, especially if they work for a government where their pay is the sweat of the outsiders. In most countries civil servants are too costly, officious, and abusive of their meager authorities. They are not necessarily overpaid but are certainly over-benefited. A civil servant in NYC receives his actual salary plus COLA during his/her entire retirement, and a US Federal employee gets 26 vacation days and 13 sick days per year. Are they better Americans than the taxpayers who pay for those benefits? This needs to be stopped since civil servants are parasites who feed on the sweat of nongovernmental affiliated workers.

WE WANT TO KNOW HOW MUCH YOU MAKE

Publish the pay benefits of the top 10 percent of any population, including the fat cats who pass as our congressmen and presidents and so on.

GET RID OF THE BUMS

An ex-American president is a nobody. If he/she was any good while in office, then the deeds will tell. Reagan, Ford, Bush I and II, and many others were really not leaders and to compensate these morons benefits other than simple retirement is immoral. Stop this before it becomes a worse problem.

HAVING A PLAN

Establish an independent agency which studies long term benefits for America. Since we are the richest country of the world, then what we do becomes global in scope. This agency would study the long term values of overmedication of Americans, the space program, the migrant worker problems, the fatal diseases such as cancer, nutrition of Americans, and other national dilemmas which seem to escape our presently "bought politicians" who sit in government at the pleasure of the richest Americans.

ISRAEL NEEDS TO PAY UP

Once Israel acknowledges the illegal disenfranchising of Palestinians, it must be forced to pay reparations.

HAS MOM OR DADDY GONE CRAZY

Nesting parents and their children must undergo yearly mental checkups, which include testing for stress and abuse of parents or children.

DOES AN APPLE A DAY KEEP THE DOCTOR AWAY

Publish and maintain a benefit/detriment list of the processes involved with foods, or the drugs we take and educate the citizenry on the science of it.

IT'S YOUR BODY RESPECT IT

Establish an independent national nutrition/medication agency, such as Consumer Report, to keep the drug makers and the inept government officials from feeding us growth hormones and drugging us into early death.

RELIGIOUS SCHOOLS

Religious schools cannot be supported by any governments, even to the point of contracting these institutions for research.

ENJOY NOW PAY LATER

Explore the possibility of having newly accepted citizens, (18 year olds), take a 7 year hiatus while being paid and furnished medical assistance. But after their 25th birthday these youths would enter the production phase of their lives and work until they die. Simply put, have them enjoy their retirement when young and then work them until they die. This will have far more merits than the present system of putting the elders in dying houses.

TEACH YOUNGSTERS ABOUT WORK

All youngsters working in places where food or drinks are handled need to be given lectures about personal hygiene. They need to be told that scratching their scalps, or their pimpled faces, or covering their mouths with their hands while sneezing and continuing on handling food, or other expelling/shedding of body solids or fluids or gasses is not allowed.

NATIONAL HEALTH INSURANCE

We have a system where we make government employees treasured assets, by providing them with excellent job security, medical insurance and retirement benefits, but for the slobs who pay these government workers, there is no such a thing as insurance, job security, or cushy retirement. Why? Establish a national health and employment insurance so that Americans are treated as humans, even if they are not employed by the governments of the land.

PEACE WEEK

Establish a week long international holiday, during which time people celebrate life and peaceful coexistence, and exchange ideas to improve the lives of those that are suffering.

PUNISH THEM AD PEOPLE

Stop the obnoxious and cancerous way of American advertising. It is unfair and uncivil to abuse people by the never ending advertisement.

CDC INTERNATIONAL

Establish an international disease control agency. Then assess the most critical diseases and spend money in finding cures and preventions.

GET WITH THE TIMES

Each country should change its national anthem on its centennial.

SPILL YOUR GUTS

Upon reaching the age of 50 every human must write down the worst and best aspects of life. Of course, provide any recommendations on how to improve things. The governments of the world will use this untraceable information to better govern people.

CRITICISM BRINGS PROGRESS

Establish debating societies where people of all ages are made to discuss problems and offer solutions.

THEM PHONY SOCCER PLAYERS

Have a sharpshooter at each soccer match. The sniper can shoot soccer players who fake injuries when playing soccer. You have seen the writhing bodies and the eyes that search for the referee to acknowledge the false sufferings. Shoot the faker after he re-enters the game and shows no short term disabilities. Use paint bullets.

COLLEGES OR SPORTS FACTORIES

Stop colleges from spending more money on their sports department than on their classics and science departments.

LET'S CHANGE THE CONSTITUTION

Establish a commission to change the US Constitution in the following areas: Take out all references to slavery; make the term of the president a single six year term; limit congressmen to serve for no longer than 10 total years; establish a single military; bar the election of blood relatives to any branch of the government; abolish the electoral college; put an age limit on the Supreme Court Justices; make it illegal for the government to refer to god in any aspect of its business, including invocations at any governmental activity, including the religious peddlers in the US Military.

DO YOU REALLY NEED TO WIPE WITH WHITE PAPER

Stop the over use of bleaching materials that go into making paper products which wind up as toilet paper, napkins, and towels. There is no sanitary gain in wiping oneself with white paper versus brown paper. You can accomplish softness and a cleaner wipe if you developed a damp brown toilet paper.

100 YEARS WITHOUT WAR

At the centennial of each country, modify the flag by adding one stripe for each decade of that country having existed in a peaceful status. Remove all stripes upon that country's entry into war, any war.

GET THEM LAWS CHANGED

Repeal all laws and treaties which treat women as unequal.

TOO MANY CONGRESSMEN

Take the ten least populated American states and unite them with nearby states. Split Texas and California to better manage them and hopefully better educate their residents.

ARE YOU TRASHY

Equip trash pickup trucks with monitoring systems so that each household is made aware of how much trash per human they generate.

BLIND BIG BROTHER

Abolish all monitoring cameras from public places.

WHO IS WATCHING ME

Make all mercantile establishments post on the entrances to the establishments a sketch of the location of their cameras or other snooping apparatus. An honest shopper should not be treated as a crook.

ARE YOU RECORDING ME

Install devices on telephones and computers that show any recording or monitoring of the user's activities.

IT'S TIME FOR LOGICAL ENGLISH

Establish an academy of American Language and please get rid of words/expressions such as: Climb down, reiterate, short circuit, power supply, I am going to be honest with you, almost, lead lead lead, and any other word or combinations thereof that must first be qualified before it can be used.

WAR IS MEN'S CHOICE, ABORTION IS WOMEN'S CHOICE

Make one and all understand that abortion, if left as a woman's choice, will most likely decrease the percentage of Americans who are in jail, on welfare, or in one way or another not trained to live in the society which caused them. Frequently remind all that as long as forgiving Christians, a majority of Americans, allow capital punishment and war, we all have blood on our hands. Abortion is just as murderous as war or capital punishment, or deaths by preventable diseases.

BLACKS AND OTHERS WERE SCREWED

Establish an Oppressed Americans Institute, funded 100% by taxpayers money, with a lifespan of at least 100 years, to transit the American blacks, women, Native Americans, from their present status into fully integrated Americans. Abolish the program the day that over 90% of these oppressed people start calling themselves Americans. Do the same in other countries where one segment of the population has been held as servant to other.

NO COMPASSION OR SOUL IN AMERICA

America has a surplus of everything but a shortage of compassion or soul. Do not be fooled by our giving aid to those whose very life we have tried to destroy with our wars. Teach Americans that killing one's family and then adopting him/her is not compassion. It is guilt.

US MILITARY IS A CANCER ON DEMOCRACY

The US military is made up of two types of people: the temporaries, who stay for one enlistment and then go on, unless they die while being used as cannon fodder. Then there are the **lifers**, who will let you know in a heartbeat that they are defending you at great sacrifice to themselves. The lifers usually become parasites to the system after their 20-30 years of military life. The post Vietnam worshipping of the military will sooner or later make these lifers believe that America really owes them something, and when that day comes, even the dumb rednecks will understand that the media was not the downfall of America, but the greed of the active/retired military was the downfall of the experiment in democracy. Start educating people about this cancer.

HELPING THE NEEDY

The time has come to establish a National Redneck Reclamation Act. (NRCA). Similar projects are needed for equally misguided sects of society in other parts of the world. This act would undo the incestuous training that somehow has tainted the minds of millions of otherwise useful Americans. Those people who consistently blame the MEDIA, the Liberals, and Homosexuals, the Supreme Court, for all that is evil in America, would be inducted into the deprogramming aspects of the Act. These people need help, their only fault is ignorance. How else can you explain a human mind so fervently adoring Christ, the first true bleeding heart liberal, and then condoning war and state executions of others? These people have a problem and they are a product of our society. They are our problem and no one else's. Help eradicate their ignorance and thus make America stronger and safer.

YOU NEED TO KNOW

Establish a National Data Center which constantly broadcasts facts about America. Again, once we do it and it is a good thing, the rest of the world will do it. Some of the interesting facts that could be on that list, based on daily, monthly, or yearly time frame:

Number of Cancer Deaths per day
Number of practicing Medical Doctors
Pounds of meat eaten daily
Number of accidental shootings daily
Number of Police officers who were not given tickets for speeding
Number of girls who impregnated themselves
Number of women beaten up by males
Number of children abused by parents
Number of practicing foaming at the mouth TV evangelists

Number of churches, synagogues, temples
Number of tax-free organizations
Total benefits, above/below the table received by politicians
Number of people on minimum wages
Number of starving people in the world
Number of obese people in the world

And all other numbers that satisfy a nation like ours, where data is debated but humanity is destroyed.

AMERICA OWNED AND OPERATED BY MIC

Last, but perhaps the worst problem facing America, is the Military Industrial Complex, (MIC). That beast exists and is draining billions of dollars from the American taxpayers and providing little if any benefit for America. Presently America has no enemies. Terrorism is a greatly exaggerated scare tactic when compared to the damages of WWII, or the simple fact that 1500 Americans die of CANCER each day. We are wasting so many billions of dollars on war gadgets that do not work, and armies which cannot fight the type of warfare which requires cops, not soldiers. The MIC has forever changed America, and we are too dumb to realize it. What progress could have been made had we invested half of the trillions that we wasted on the military, into medical research? The list of our worst enemies, in order of their damage are: Ignorance, Religion, and MIC. Solve the MIC problem by making people understand that we have been robbed of trillions of taxpayers' dollars by politicians and greedy CEOs, while these bastards scared us with created enemies.

In case You missed the Point

Women, Mothers and all who care about the human race, it's time for you to assume a lifetime responsibility for the product that you make and to insure that it is not used to destroy the lives and hopes of other humans or nature.

To do that, you need to convince men that you are equal to them, if not better.

In case you missed the point, look at this simple fact:

1500 Americans are buried everyday because Cancer, the real terrorist, killed them. Should we, the most advanced nation so far, in the course of humanity, be fighting this real and non dis-criminating terrorist versus sending your children to die in other countries fighting made up foes?

Whatever you decide to do is your choice, but please tell your daughters that they are more than the silent makers of the most critical raw material of the next war.

Tell your daughters that the only reason men are in charge is because women failed to control their destiny.

Thank you.

www.ingramcontent.com/pod-product-compliance
Lightning Source LLC
Chambersburg PA
CBHW061220280526
45784CB00006B/2558